Cold Blue Roses

poems by Evan Myquest
R.L. Crow Publications, 2020

Cold Blue Roses
copyright © 2020 by Evan Myquest
first printing

All rights reserved.
Printed in the United States of America.
No part of this book may be reproduced
in any manner whatsoever without written
permission except in the case of brief quotations
embodied in critical essays and articles.

Acknowledgements –
Various forms of some of these poems
have previously appeared in:

WTF, Medusa's Kitchen, Dangerous Goods,
Convergence, Sacramento News and Review,
Sacramento Poetry Center anthology "Late Peaches,"
Sacramento Voices, Primal Urge,
Little M Press libretto "On the Occasion of a Performance
at the Shine Café.

Front cover art by Peter Wedel
Cover design by R.L. Crow Publications

R.L. Crow Publications
P.O. Box 262
Penn Valley, CA 95946
U.S.A.

ISBN: 978-0-9971780-3-6
Library of Congress Control Number: 2020944703

This book is dedicated to:
Anyone leaving it better than they found it,
and the parents who raised them that way,
especially "Doc" and Audrey.

Contents –

Miles Davis Plays	1
Curlylocks	2
Happy Dancing Matilda	3
A Hole in the Hum	4
Coffeehouse Music Man	5
Churro Love	6
How Now	7
For the Little One Stuck in the Hospital	8
Insomniacs, Bohannon on the Case	10
The Sixteenth Minute of Fame	12
Overnight Success	13
Got It at the Pre-Life Auction	14
Self-Worth	15
My Two Lane	16
Stockholm Syndrome in My Country	18
Threads	19
Toward the Manhattan of Anthills	20
Daring the Demons	21
Church of the Low Expectations	22
Sleeping with Dogs	24
Dibs on Bibs	25
Dogs of War	26
The Universe Factory Tour	28
Hey Shooter	29
Coffeehouse Memories	30
Gremlins	31
Honey, Take It to the Bank	32
I Met an Old Woman and She Said	34

The Inherited Painting	35
Kissing the Waiting Area Carpet	36
Junk Science Genesis for the Hobbyist	37
The Night I Dreamt I was Sarah Palin	38
Little Poem	40
Love the Funny Looking Birds at the Zoo	41
A Mystery Poem	42
Nested Naps	43
Have to Dig Him Up Again	44
My Old Man Stash	45
The Flight	46
Love and Memories in the Future Fire	47
Play Diamonds for Me Sam	48
Rudi the Feather-Kid	49
Scraps	50
Secured Away	51
Electric Sparrows Murmur to Me in the Trees	52
Then in My Nightmare	53
Thoughts and Prayers	54
What We Know	56
Cheering for the Tall Ones	57
The Cowboy and the Vampire	58
Dance You	59
Elevation Contours of the Split Oreo Dunk	60
Pickle Dancer	61
The Green Burial People ...	62
Holiday, with Remembered Scent ...	64
It Happened in Vegas	65

Spending the Day with a Fine Thought	66
When You Consider Yourself Learned	68
Left in the Lurch	70
Music Box Ballerina	71
My Vincent Price Dream	72
Out with the Old – Never Really Happens	73
Procrastination Marks	74
Pickup Line	76
Snail Shakespeare	77
They'd Have You Believe	78
Why in Hell – Yerington Nevada	80
The Trade	82
All Donations Accepted	83
After Hours Bond Girl	84
Nothing but a Number	86
An Anthropological Apology	87
Balloons	88
Bar Talk in B	89
How to Keep a Friend	90
Boney Maroney, Sloopy and ...	91
The Callback	92
Bar Talk in D	93
Mid-Life Punk	94
Bookie Blues	95
Bus Ride Next To an Unfettered Mind	96
The Wish	97
Bike Rider Pedaling into Tomorrow	98

Cold Blue Roses

Miles Davis Plays

Jazzbo baby
devil in a diaper
horns on head
does not play well with others
until late in life
grim murder of status quo
the chalk outline
goes forever.

Curlylocks

Sweet banana curled wife and darling
we sleep in spoon drawer formation
I feel the crawling sensation as
those long tresses fall or creep over my ears
from your pillow as you snore.

I brush them away and yet they return
springy soft and childishly elegant
that curling iron whimsical creation.

Now they pull my lips back and block my cries
how is it that you smile so beatific
as those slinky things do their worst
my eyes bulge as my throat feels the pressure
yet for softness your skin outdoes the silk of your slip
my fingers are bloody from trying to undo the noose
your constrictor locks perpetrate
perhaps this is a dream
perhaps this is imagined.

In the morning
please let me sleep in
I feel so short of life right now
and must try to close my eyes
glad I did not wake you
with my thrashing.

Happy Dancing Matilda

Our love is the dancing elephant
in the room making the cat nervous
its tail twitching
running from under one chair to another
with each footfall and thump.
Our love is the thundering herd
making the cat nervous.
Our love is the giant mouse
making the cat watchful.
Our love is the bounding mastiff
eye to eye with the cat, under the couch
making him – uneasy
but then our love is a warm lap
and the cat curled, purring
oblivious to the imaginary menagerie
wasting its menace in his dreams.

A Hole in the Hum

If there's ever
five minutes of silence
in the conversation
that's me joining in
doing my share.
I'm smart enough to know
I can't compete with
intelligent silence.
People say silence is heavy.
Well, how heavy can it be
if it only takes a word to
disturb it
shatter it to pieces?
How heavy can it be
if a pin drop is its undoing?
A vow of silence is
wasted if sandaled footfalls
slap on the monastery floor.
Even the rude vesper quarter
bells of towered Big Ben are
programmed to interrupt
the sublime on
the quarter hour.

Coffeehouse Music Man

You asked for requests
so
I want to hear
that song
with the doo dah dee dee
wah wah
and the part about the wheelchair
and the cat's tail
and the people with their
hair on fire.
You sang it once at that place on L St. last year.

Oh, so that's the name?
What does that have to do with anything
in the song?
You expect me to remember a title
you never ever even uttered before singing it?
Sorry that the clever cd names escape me
maybe I will remember next time.

How about the one
with the guy from
the Rolling Stones in it instead?
You know
doo doo
da doo doo
woo-ooo.

Churro Love

The
ballgame
vendor
knows
me
by
now.
Knows
my
weakness
for the
tall,
thin
sugar
coated
sweetest
things
in the
cheap
seats
that
I can
afford.

How Now

So why is it necessary to tax
what almost everyone lacks?
Instead, tax animals in zoos and on farms and such
where they lie about and get fed so overly much.

So cough up now brown cow and dumb ox
I suppose we'll not catch the quick brown fox
but that lazy dog
we'll tax to the hilt his sleepy fog.

For the Little One Stuck in the Hospital

Hey little one, they're going to fix you right up
well not right up right this minute
you might have to stay a night or two or more
since that's when "they" work –
(don't worry because you are never alone)
all those happy slap-tail beavers in their yellow hardhats
looking over midnight construction plans
as they string flood lights and fences
they unload from trucks
beeping their (watch out) back up beeps.

There's no limit to the kinds of honking and noise
that happens as you sleep and you don't even hear a beep
hand waves from red bandana worker beavers
to white bandana trucker beavers
leaning out their driver windows.
They move their trucks around to dump all that scaffolding
put it around you and yes it might take a while
to get all that going.

The boss beaver in his orangey hardhat studies the plans
he makes hurried chich-chich-chich sounds
into his walkie-talkie
which means wait stop-stop-stop
then it is chich-chich-chich all okay to go-go-go
move here, move there
and yell louder, okay that's good, that's just right.
We need more light, and lights go on everywhere
like a whirling bunch of musical carnival rides
dot-dot-dotta-de-dot-dot-dee
a whole construction carnival with lots of slapping tails
and high fives

but when the busy beavers start adding towering new floors
and hanging your glamorous new doors
it won't be long until the whistle blows – break time!
You can bet they have accomplished plenty
even though it seems to you like it's taking forever –
they turn the page on the plans and
before you know it there are more trucks and
the lights, and more new floors high in the air
all for you
all for the little one who thinks they're stuck and
they're the only one in the room
when there are hundreds of busy beavers
running lighted elevators up and down, and
moving crane booms with a hundred lights on each of them
into place.

You, the lucky one.
That boss beaver knows his stuff
you're going to get up and fly away in no time now
you will get to make noise and play with toys
he promises that!
Whatever you do--don't say a word
if your doctor turns around to walk away and his tail peeks
out of his coat
and you hear him
go chich-chich-chich down the hall.

Insomniacs, Bohannon on the Case

My suffering insomniac friends.
Science says the requirement for sleep is
an empty head. A zen no-mind
coupled with self-hypnotic triggers
to take advantage of the void.
I know most of you are adept at this
empty-headedness.
Maybe quite accomplished at the practice.

Let me offer some help to the uneasy wakeful.
Imagine as you lie there unable
to clear your mind, see that there is now
an antique Colt pistol pushed to your ear
by the reigning cowboy badass of TV land.

I do not suggest a zombie gang
of "Ponderosa Cartwrights." That is far
too entertaining for our required effect.

We want a lone wolf type.
I'm thinking Cullen Bohannon with a temper.
Yes, the "Hell on Wheels" TV badass guy.

So Cullen says to you in your mind
clear your head, or I'll clear it for you.
He means business. He's had it with
your tossing and turning and dumb dialectic thoughts.
You don't sleep, then he doesn't sleep.
Simple. That's just modern science.

In your mind you have to resolve that
this guy is a big dot credible threat. You need this
authority with a six shooter to convince you
to sleep. No argument allowed cocked Colt-wise.

Those racing dancing dharma thoughts hour after hour
lingering with complexity humor and wit
you pride yourself on. ...Toast.

Soon only the name of the man
will be necessary to badger away that sleep deprivation.
A mantra of gunslinger no-mind on the name alone.
Cullen. Cullen. Cullen. Yo, Bohannon.   O Cullen.

Remember, no zombie heroes of yesteryear.
No zombie Roy or singing zombie Gene. Or zombie Duke.
We will consider a young make-my-day Eastwood
The I got your limitations right here guy.
A worthy authority figure for our purposes.

But no honky-tonk piano playing Bronco Billy action.
I hope this advice works as well for you
as it does for me. I find empty-headedness
a therapeutic requirement for daily existence.
Sleep as well.
Have a nice threat.
Sweet dreams.

The Sixteenth Minute of Fame

It got awful quiet.
Where did everyone go?
I don't think I changed.
You were so attentive
so appreciative.
We were like family
we swore eternal love
nothing could separate us.
Our thing, so deep.
Where did
everyone go?

Overnight Success

In the way a celebrity
in harm's way from bad choices
wants to pull back
but doesn't have the knack

one less resistant to the pull
of the perilous ledge

call it the intended consequence
of millions of fans
yelling "jump"
then rushing to buy magazines
barely out of bundles.

Got It at the Pre-Life Auction

Mr. Auctioneer
on the item list today
number four billion
eight hundred thirty five million
two hundred fifty four thousand
six hundred forty five.

Yes
that one
the one on the
blue marble planet.

Yes, that one.
I want to be born to that eightieth percentile
high quality of life, educated, rich dirt country
small town nuclear family.
Tom Sawyer river and caves playground
baseball and peanuts
as a healthy
accountant to be.

No starvation
no pressure
no soldiering
a darling little niche existence
on the blue marble.

I bid that one
how lucky do I need to be
Norway?
wait…the part about
baseball and peanuts.

Self-Worth

I heard that in the third world
you can send two of your kids to college
for a liver or kidney.
Well, my eyeballs went
to HBO last night
after I finished the newspaper
I pledged PBS
my brain for a tote bag.
I could afford that since
usage levels have been declining
and with shelf-life deterioration what it is
I had to let my ears
go to Apple for a song.

Perhaps some day
the returns will be better
but a market is a market
and like land
they're not making more of me
worth buying.

Perhaps they'll keep me alive
for my dwindling attention span alone
at least I can afford to pay attention
that has to be worth an As Seen On TV
pot washing pill
so call today only
and receive not one but two
great college educations
and then get to chat with the nice couple
on that global shopping network
about Joe the neighbor
who clued me in on their bargain of the day
for only three easy monthly payments.

My Two Lane

Revealed by morning's light
down my country two lane

about a mile down
past the meadow culvert bridge
before the turn-off
a speed limit sign along my commute
has been murdered.

One morning there was a small dent
a mar of the paint.

During the next month
several dents
then more mornings pass
to reveal larger dents
with paint peeled away.

The week before the sign was replaced
a half-dollar sized hole gaped through the steel
in the morning light.

Makes me wonder
about all the shots
that missed.

Not much farther down
a lone tree is also under attack
ten feet off the road
without another for a mile or more
minding its own long life.

Morning lights revealed
within a year the scars of
three single drivers' deaths
under its boughs.

Somewhere the word is out
those afflicted by surrender know
how to beat the insurance company.

I bet the life
and casualty companies
will confer and petition
the old tree's demise.

As for the sign
and the two lane road
no one can say
death is unacquainted
with this far corner
of the map.

Stockholm Syndrome in My Country

What a lovely vacation
Wish you were here
Stockholm, sort of Sweden
Volvo country no cowboys –
I hear they have a lot of hostages.
How else could they derive
a local syndrome?

I think I must be in Stockholm at times
since I tolerate the new leader
when I suppose I should resent the despot
and my captivity.

They (no names please) say it is not captivity
if you love your captors.
Is that denial or a defense mechanism?
Can't live with them
Can't shoot them
from prison.

Threads

Once I pulled on a thread
and pulled
and pulled
a long thread
I pulled and
I pulled.
First there was a little pile
of thread
then there was a big pile
of thread
I pulled and
pulled more.
My fingers got tired
then my arms
but still the thread came along.
I don't know why the sweater
did not unravel.
Now, for some reason
I can't find my wife
anywhere
or my street
my relatives
my ancestors
and now I am in a swamp.
There are dinosaurs around.
Do you suppose
time really is
a fabric
and
pardon me
but you have this thread
hanging.
Let me get that
for you.

Toward the Manhattan of Anthills

If I was an ant from a small colony –
taking a break from the busy
looking at the Manhattan of anthills
a foot (a human foot) over
I would applaud (in a human way)
the amount of peaceful cooperation
going in such a non-peaceful way.

If I wiggle my antennae in approval of them
and take their "kiss offs"
in a non-offensive, affirmative (human) way
well, I can afford a little
self-satisfaction in the exchange.

And in not giving away the location
of the cookie crumbs behind our village hill –
throw a kiss off-back to them
in the sweetest
(human finger) way.

Daring the Demons

Like children
calling a mountain lion
here kitty
do they worship devils
with wishes so dark.

Kids
when you knock over those gravestones
even in the light of day
do you know the end
of the game you play
as lurking
demons
snap to air sniffing attention
at the pained sound of the defiled.

Defiant children
here kitty-kitty
and comes the lion maned demon

for their skin, and salty oils
uninclined to let them keep
their faces or their souls
because the vandals
forget
it is always midnight
somewhere.

Church of the Low Expectations

Looking at life in thirds
twenty-five years at a time.
That's twenty-five years of
ridiculously high expectations
while young and idealistic.
The second twenty-five
the advent of realism with
strength and health.
Then comes the third twenty-five –
you know where this is going –
low and lower go the expectations
low and lower goes the strength and health
low and lower goes the ambition
low and lower – you get the idea.
Life is ready to take you under
no matter the planning
no matter the resources
life has extended a message –
lower your expectations or the
depression will get you no matter how
you bargain with fate
you deny it
you fight it
then it happens
you join the church
of low expectations.
The world is right again with low expectations
the lower the better you're informed.
Welcome! This is the good part.
Enjoy the sacraments of achievement sans effort.
Enrollment is automatic.
Be a stripper – shed those expectations
like break-away pants flung off knobby knees.
No one believes
you even have expectations

given the time you have left.
They're ready to leave you alone in the desert.
No bothering, no burdens.
They will avoid the discussion of
your clothes
your attitude
your negativity
your final wishes.
After all
you're not part of the game anymore.
No more searching for the point
there's no expectation of finding it.
After all, a search is just an expectation
you've made it to the sanctuary
of low expectations.
Sweet spot
like an observation tower.
Like the cheap seats where no one else
is even sure if you're rooting for the team anymore.
Cool
so cool.
Church is in session
and no surprise.
The bells sound beautiful.
Do whatever you like
it's not like anyone is expecting
anything of you.

Sleeping with Dogs

What do you want me to say before coffee?
The world is a crummy, lousy, a no good place?

Injustice everywhere, society without morals
workplace subjugation indenture, ethnic bigotry
racial profiling, creeping totalitarianism ...
The list does go on.

Wake me when the news is good
I won't be hard to find.
I will be hiding under the bed
begging the dog
not to give me away.

Dibs on Bibs

Napkin on floor.
Food on my shirt.
No one ever asks what was for lunch
Instead they say:
Looks like that roast beef was juicy.
Looks like mustard and onions on that dog.
Looks like a side of mashed, or, something.
Looks like there was room for dessert today.
I am what I eat and
I wear what I eat.
Oh wide ties
please come back in fashion soon.
My laundry gets far more calories than me.

Dogs of War

Relax.
The dogs are coming
unchain the war machine that has no quit
they hold on, they hate peace
they love destruction
they bite their chains
they bite the hands that bred them
fed them
they talk isolation and jump the next troop ship
talk about your heat seekers
not to worry
fetch, sic, rip – to shreds.
If offered a dog bowl of the best dogfood
they would rather take
the hand that brought it.

Wake them
watch them sniff the air.
Heads whipping for the source.

They come loping –
they come loping
metal dogs
metal shoot first gas
and sonic and flash, and computer
weaponry.
The dogs – they have it all
and we have them.

Remember
when the collar comes off
there's no putting it back
until the streets run

not with blood
but with the blast furnace magma
of the street itself.
Take care –
over here
over there.

The Universe Factory Tour

They said it is all the same universe
we knew better
we had been to the factory
they were turning them out in very large "globes" or "gobs"
by very large numbers.
I bet you want to know who the surprise 'they' are
and the surprise 'where' the factory is.
There is a thing you sign before the tour.
Sorry, "No one can tell."

It is strange to think of a factory
with a shift whistle and all that fusioning and fissioning
turning out universes on a moving line
after all, one eats a particular dessert and never imagines
a candy factory flowing with rivers of caramel, does one?
Almost overwhelming was the urge
to snatch one from the winding line
to take a souvenir globe home for the mantel
of course the baby universes were not fully expanded yet
think bonsai versions of compressed galaxies
but inflatable like an airplane escape slide
just pour in the extra magical nothingness and stand back
to experience the practical everything-ness.

I imagine myself as this speck
in a globe, on a mantel
wishing someone, or something,
would dust more.

Hey Shooter

I want to know something about you
after all you changed the course of history.
For instance:
Did you like going on vacation
or out for holiday fireworks?
Did you like swimming on hot days?
Did you have a few dollars on you?
Did it seem like the smart choice after all?
Are there people who wanted to do what you did
but aren't impressed by you?
Do you hear from them?

Are you what your name now represents?
Are you worried reporters will stop coming?
Did you have a favorite teacher?
Did you ever try to learn a second language?
Did you have a lover? I mean
did you have pictures in your wallet?
Did you have an idea or just an opportunity?
What was your IQ, just a ballpark guess
when you got the idea?
What thought gave yourself permission to do it?
What do you think of the clever conspiracy rumors?
What were you originally going to do
with the rest of your life?
What surprises might your autopsy reveal?
What was last Christmas like for you?
Are you satisfied with the name recognition?
Who got your car?
Who was supposed to have your back?
If a person from the future
took you somewhere for a beer instead
would you have minded?

Coffeehouse Memories

Nikki Sudden's
at True Love Cafe
his bandmate's singing
a Jackpot song
sure –
and TV Smith's
touring with Doctor Frank
and Kevin's opening –
you're so dreaming.

Yeah, and in the dream
they did a 23 hour Anton scene
c'mon –
and I suppose Jerry slept on the doorway floor.

Yes, yes –
oh BS – if that happened
then they'd put a plaque right there
inside such a hallowed door
– and have a bald-headed man
sell midnight waffles to tourists.
Now that –
that's a dream.

Gremlins

At the foot of the bed
gremlins with incredible glee
stretch each other to almost two-dimensional wonder
to scare children
into bad dreams and awakened parents.

As the parents wipe eyes
wondering what now
the gremlins run for cover

lights go on
gremlins hide and snicker
children get told about telling tales

and no matter how well they explain
the sights they've seen
they're told how it's just a dream.

It is not fair
gremlins get all the fun
because as soon as the room is newly dark
it turns back into
the gremlins' amusement park.

Honey, Take It to the Bank

It was so long ago yet remains so easy to recall
a first kiss so sweet it stunned the mind
turned knees to jelly
so shy I could not believe it happened

that electric moment
of fumbling intent

now
so many more moments
in our treasure of friends.

Funerals have come our way
scant outweighed by the many births celebrated
though we take life in its circles
with congratulating hugs (and tears)
with consoling hugs (and tears).

That first kiss was a staircase
of the senses:

a degree
a diploma
a tasseled hat high in the air

a reason to swagger
a reason to walk head held high
a reason to choose more roads untraveled.

How I wish that first kiss
was with you
but love, this I guarantee

my last gentle falling kiss will be yours and
it will be the best by miles and years in recall
the best by miles and years in recall.

I Met an Old Woman and She Said
(for Ruth Gordon)

She said the stars were bigger before the war.
I said, "the movie stars?"
She said, "No, young man (which made me look around)
the night sky stars.
They were bigger.
Much brighter than now."

She said the stars became even bigger
when they started to talk.
I said, "Oh, when sound came to the movies?"
She said, "No, when the night sky would whisper about love
in my ear."

She said stars don't dance the way they used to.
I said, "No more Astaire. No more Kelly and O'Connor ..."
She said, "No, the stars in the night sky and I
used to samba across the heavens
like it was Carnival the night through."

She said the stars aren't what they used to be.
I said, "When the Golden Age of movies died out?"
She said, "No, when the stars in the night sky deserted us
for more appreciative and younger lovers."

She said stars don't kiss like they used to.
I said, "The great romance idols, Valentino and Novarro..."
She said, "No, no, the night sky used to come down
and make love to me.
Alas, no more."

She said the stars were better dressed in black and white.
I said, "Before all the satellite telescope pictures?"
She said, "No, silly, in those old, great films.
The ones you call 'movies'."

The Inherited Painting

High up on the high wall
of our bedroom
there is a painting of a pastoral
grove in sunshine.
It is a nice expressionist piece
that we love very much.
I remember first seeing it
at my late in-laws' house
in its prominent living room place.
It seemed more at home in their house
but they are gone and the house
belongs to other people now
and the painting, well, we have
given it a good home even though
we did not buy it, did not decide to
sacrifice other niceties to own it
did not agree that it was too
amazing not to own it
did not congratulate each other
on acquiring it – hanging it so prominently
it is more a piece of the past
than an artwork we had to have above all.
And yet, there is a chain of ownership
we are proud to acknowledge and
we are proud to love it for the extra reasons
that go with missing loved ones.
But today, after thirty years
we talk about it as a fantastic piece of art.
Like we were the lucky original acquirers.
Like it chose our wall after decades
of others' appreciation.
We talk about it like we had seen it first
brought it home first
hung it first, and studied it first, inch by inch.
Then loved it, inch by inch, first.

Kissing the Waiting Area Carpet

Public address announcement
in the San Diego
departure lounge
for Chicago
due to severe snow and ice in Chicago
our San Diego to Chicago flight is cancelled.
Please see the service desk
for alternate arrangements.

I have never heard
a louder spontaneous crowd
cheer
in my life.

The announcement continued
all San Diego to Chicago flights are
overbooked for two days.

Another cheer and
there is a God or two after all
not one angry soul.

I love when people get it.

Junk Science Genesis for the Hobbyist

She asked, what was that big bang
I heard coming from the garage?
He said, just a little backfire.
I was backing out the new project.
Nothing to worry about.
So she didn't and went about her apple polishing.
He said, the new project was going well enough
what with the pistons pistoning and the spheres sphering.
She said, you will neaten up after you're finished, right?
He added, there won't be a trace I assure you dear.
Then he remembered that primordial ooze
on the garage floor.
But didn't mention it to her – no need to agitate mother.
He said, would you like to see what I've been working on?
She said, maybe later dear that noise just bothered me.
Time to clean up a little, he thought
as the small planet Pluto shot past the window behind her.

The Night I Dreamt I was Sarah Palin

You say there are happy days ahead
when the sun shines bright on old Kentucky homes.
You say there are bluebirds and blinding white snow peaks
where the chirpy songs and mountain majesty reigns.

If you say it's good for me, then it must be
my body's twelve way salvation
to get me the billboard eyes
of the world's best models looking my way.
Man, I am so going to vote for you next election.

Of course we do not want to change a thing
my vote is for sale
the check is in the mail, isn't it
and my new patio set is on order
how much more right can things get
with such mountains' majesty?
Waiter, give me two more bowls of whatever he's having.
I am taking your word for everything at face value
no discounted wonderment.

It is about time prosperity reared its ugly head around here
I was beginning to think the world was going to hell
in a basket.
Ring the bells, ring the bells, ring the bells
ring the hallelujah bells.

People are sleeping all over.
Last night must have been a good time.
Look how tired we are, how exhausted
we are –
how ready to wake from the nightmare
man, that was something
how that commie Russia was growing fangs.

That Fu Manchu had the guy pumped full of poison darts
I thought Peter Cushing would never show up
to shove a cross in that Lee guy's face
we were doomed in dungeons
with Vincent Price in cardinal robes.

Screaming in my sleep I was
trying to wake all of you
and here I was the one asleep.
You say you and I must believe
head for the ski resorts for a cocoa adjustment
head for the beaches for a nap under a striped umbrella
wait
i saw those movies too
wasn't there a snow creature with fangs
wasn't there a shark that ate all the kids
and the cop had to warn everyone
but the mayor said go back to sleep.
It's all right, it was a dream
dude are you wearing polyester
and weren't the bank's doors
locked yesterday during working hours.
What's that about?
What time is the soup on at the dole-a-rama kitchen.
We had better get going
the line could be long today
nice shaking your hand, buddy
you got my vote.

Little Poem

We had two finches
R2 and D2
little birds
little names.
Loved 'em
like baby elephants.

Love the Funny Looking Birds at the Zoo

They're all colors
and shapes of feet, wing and bill.

Blessed with Mother Nature's palette
feathery rainbow plumage
laughably limbed.
Birds of the gooney walk
and looney cry.

But still, were I bug-sized
I'd be running like hell.

A Mystery Poem

The aliens that abducted my best friend
left traces behind
like his occupied house
his working phone
his desk at work with his likeness still on the job.
This clone even drives the same car
cleverly takes the same route to his job everyday.
He hangs with these false friends in bars, too.
Goes to the same restaurants
uses the same drycleaner
his pantry is restocked with all his favorite foods.
The phony uses the same toiletries and cologne
has the same prescriptions in his medicine cabinet.
I'm afraid they will get away with this
so I have decided to abduct the clone
then they will listen to me.
The clone won't be able to signal the ship again.
I have this all documented, full video.
I'm not fooling around.
Either they bring my friend back
or I waste their pod guy.

Nested Naps

I lay down for a quick nap
soon asleep
dreaming of dreaming of taking a quick nap.
I woke up from the first dream
didn't know how long I'd slept.
There was a new moon out
and snow that wasn't there before.
In this dream I ran for the nearest newspaper
which was dated a decade after I went to sleep.
A youngster ran by very fast calling me Grandpa.
No grandkid I knew.
So much confusion I thought I must be dreaming.
Which ended that dream as I took a turn for the lucid
but in this dream it was ten years earlier
and I needed a nap
only a quick one
because the grandkid had worn me out
with the sledding and dog chasing through the snow.
Wait. What dog?
We only have a cat.
An old cat that just sleeps in the sun.
No, sorry, that's me. The cat. Sleeping in the sun.
What a dream in a dream.
I'm hungry.
Where is that old man with my food?
There. Sleeping, again.

Have to Dig Him Up Again

If I had one friend in the world
it was him
but
friends sometimes fall out
over the silliest things.
Like if one gets abducted by aliens
and gets laughed at
by a certain friend.
How to explain?
I was abducted not from Earth
but to Earth
I had to unmask to show him
then I had to kill him and bury him
to keep my secret.
But damned if he didn't
have my car keys in his pocket.

My Old Man Stash

You are not going to believe this.
All my drugs have become legal.
Then, on top of that, someone else
pays for them.
I now sort them into a tray box
in daily and hourly intake requirements.
Legally, they come in the mail
across state lines and everything
overnight.

Who wants me so happy
and where were they
forty years ago?

The Flight

Do I have to hear
do I have to see
must time pass
must I feel
to have my sense of you?

The plane
flies with us
first class as always
we buckle in
oxygen masks above us
for shortness of breath
should we linger over kisses

forget to breathe
as we leave our bodies
make astral love
lose sight
lose hearing
lose time itself
catch flight after flight
while holding hands
to board again.

Love and Memories in the Future Fire

Many years ago, when I posed for that picture
I should've thought
"Someday I am going to look so young in this picture."
I also should've thought
"Man, these clothes are going to look so old
but rocking cool."
Many years ago, when I proudly posed
for that picture
I should've thought
"There'll be a day this beautiful car won't exist
and neither will the dealership behind it."
Many years ago, when we posed
for our prom picnic picture
I should've thought
"It is going to be piercing hell
to point out the friends passed."
Many years ago, when I posed for my cap and gown picture
I should've thought
I'm going to miss that guy taking this picture.
Many years past, and from a better time
should I have thought
"Many years from now
will I think of the girl in the gown and
wonder who is the guy in the tux
with all those beer and drink glasses?"
When we sat for that wedding picture
shouldn't we have thought, without doubt –
"Damn we sure were right to think we were right
for each other."
Why didn't I think "It's going to be so miraculous
just to share all the coming years with you."

Play Diamonds for Me Sam
                    (for Scott Wannberg)

A mind of diamonds like a waterfall
in the land of the tall Black dancers.
"Quartermain" finding the lost African mine
with each verse.

A mind of diamonds like a waterfall
taking plunder on the seas of her majesty
the Jolly Roger over Errol Flynn or Captain Jack
mocking Davy Jones
with each verse.

A mind of diamonds like a waterfall
in world of black shadow where
the spaghetti cowboy's eyes take all the light and
guns blaze everywhere as the dingus and
the private eyes meet the "Fat Man" and Lorre.
The detective avenges his partner
with each verse.

But a mind of diamonds like a waterfall
cannot last forever like those on the screen.
You were always front row at the theater
where the diamonds were kept.
Like Stewart Granger, you brought them back to us
with each verse.

Rudi the Feather-Kid

Our bird flies from his house
his cage is always open.
Then the little dive bomber
sits on the couch with us
and stares into our eyes.
It's a winning strategy
for a peanut or an oyster cracker
or late night microwave popcorn
zooming out at the sound of the popping.
Every once in a while
usually in the quiet
of a book reading afternoon
He sits on one of us
and just ... falls asleep.

Scraps

The sense of hearing
something between the lines
something between
the riffs and refrains
the bridge and
the finish.
A couple notes
juxtaposed
that vibrated
into a feeling
a years old remarkably
familiar feeling
of radio songs
and certain cars
and good times
down country roads
what played
when you were first alive
what played when you first
wore that dress
in the picture or
when you were married
when the little ones came
those times
you had the problems
whatever they played
whatever song's hook
stayed embedded.
Thank you music.
Thanks again and again
for the wonderful scraps
that fill the books
never bound.

Secured Away

Under lock
and key
miles down
in a granite
vault
a tiny kiss waits
for when
you're not
looking.

Electric Sparrows Murmur to Me in the Trees

The great honking butterfly migration
in the sky when the seasons change
the drones come back to Capistrano
we will duck for cover
the whirlybirds have it in for us
they take to the rafters
they nest in the bus stop shelters.
If it weren't for the music they offer
and the morning news
from perches in trees
weather reports at stoplights
I'd rather they recharged off other roofs
coops and grids
and stop the hovering at my door.

With the latest sales pitches on the way to my car
the social media "paparazzi volanti"
are embarrassing at times
when they let the world know what ice cream I like
and how uninteresting my life really is
much as they disguise themselves
as the hallowed swallows emulated
or goldfinches, sparrows, and what have you.
I could do with a bit less of movie
and theater previews and be
much more grateful for the "happy birthday, sir – madam."
A lot less of the "how's that prescription working out"
The increasing twitter
of fitness jogging and dieting affirmations.
The acrobatic murmurations we face are ingenious after all –
especially when they flare out for
the smoothie sponsorship logo
while I hear Tom Lehrer singing
"Poisoning Pigeons in the Park."

Then in My Nightmare

Painters without room at home have sunlit studios.
I see musicians with high tech sound recording rooms.

Long ago the writer's backyard shed
or attic garret was part of my life.
Solitude in search of the words to reflect the world
sending distraction to the boundaries of my self-confinement.

Whatever it was, it worked – self-exiled days were done.
What wouldn't one give for those productive days?
To not be forever on the phone about the appearances
performances and the marketing.

As the entourage grows from agent to publicist
photographer to lawyer to graphic artists
and certainly the makeup woman, and clerking intern
demanding time and room
for the secretary and computer tech.

Which reminds me, it probably started
with pen and paper.
Is there room in the budget
for those old items after all the helpers
helping this artist find where in that crowd
my muse got lost.
A Marx Brothers shipboard stateroom
if ever there was one.

Thoughts and Prayers

The woods are full of them
throw a rock hit one scampering by
I will bet you also swim
in thoughts and prayers.
My basement is knee deep in them
it isn't that they're cheap
though they do pop out of thin air
with the slightest concentration
heavy with sincerity
light with uselessness.

As for a delivery system
pack this payload of sympathy
into the nose cone
of a simple hallmark gesture
and send twenty bucks to a charity
for balance.

It's pretty common to spread them
like flower petals before a lucky couple
marbles before the pallbearer parade.
Often, I will recommend pea shooting straws
votive paper planes
rubber band zip guns primed and ready
Jack In The Boxes on the last note
of "pop goes the weasel."
Put them in envelopes in place of glitter
fill trunks of driverless cars full
burn them for winter fuel

pay them forward in place of chocolates
recharge your car for extra mileage.
Take them with water to sleep through the night.
Best of all, gobble them like M&M trail mix
on long drives. Shower and body wash.
Wax and polish the car out in the drive.
Rinse between applications.
Thoughts and prayers.
Who knew how useful?

What We Know

At my age I still fall in love with you
several times a day.
When the sun casts your shadow
I want it to overlap mine. When hands are held
can it have been this long together?
So much unsaid
if we ever had to say all those things
with more than a nod or wave of the hand
it would take the eons of the world.
So much is unsaid, often at a cost of understanding
but not as much as the time we would lose
answering
I know
I know.

Of course we know where we agree
though it never hurts to keep saying I love you.
How I would imagine
how I would hurt
if the world took you away
before our time should end.
When the last words we say to each other
will be
I know
I know
me too.

Cheering for the Tall Ones

I want the tall trees to take it all back
whether the earth wants to push up new continents
or become the smoothest sphere sanded by wind and flood
neither ice nor Eden for a blanket
I want the marks and fissures to balance out
and the tallest come back to rule
I want the ingredients back to make it come true
air and earth free of the killing acid, salt and heat
water fresh and pure cycling around the planet
let my bones nourish the tallest
or even the sprouts of the giants
that and that alone gives the lie shame
the loudest defilers were to have dominion
the greatest inhabitants never made a sound
except for their dying fall
their last imprint on my existence
I want the quiet towering giants
to take it all back
turning to unbothered stone
in their own time.

The Cowboy and the Vampire

I said to the vampire
across my campfire
"I don't want to be impolite
but I hope you haven't stopped for a
bite."

In his eastern euro way he asked
what I was having this break
I looked up from my whittling and said
"steak?"
Seems last I saw my uninvited guest
he was fast headed
way more west.

Dance You

I want to dance you to the breakfast table
I want to dance you to your car
I want to dance you to your work desk.
When you come home
I want to dance you to the dinner table
in my arms
stepping lightly
thinking of you
full minded of the shortness of life.
I want to dance you wherever and whenever
you leave me and you return.
There is memory in dance
that cannot fade.
The touch of you
is the sum and the forgetting of problems.
It is the concentration and focus
of the two of us.
In dance –
in the dance
in the memory of the dance
I want to dance you
as slow as possible.
Later
we will twist and shout.

Elevation Contours of the Split Oreo Dunk

The lab had all the gear in place.
On one side of the two-way mirror
the observation team and invited VIPs
everyone ready for the countdown.
Lead Engineers and Senior Engineers
were texting standby warnings.
A milky splashdown expectation in mind.
On the other side of the mirror
the bespectacled kid wasn't paying attention.
All he could think of was the frosting in the middle
and the deft twist that would expose it.

Pickle Dancer

Stopped at a long red light
the air conditioning up high
I see him full motion.
He's dancing in a pickle suit.

Why I don't know
beyond the pay
I'm sure the answer is layered.
I wish his sign said something
I could understand dancing about
a newborn, a lottery win
a very good wager.

This is probably better work in the winter
not as good now, in the humid summer.
If I was desperate I would do this too
but at my advanced age
the pickling process is underway.

While I don't sign dance on street corners
I can relate
to the sourly disposed.
The dancing looks like good exercise.
Something I could use.

I will pray to St. Vitus
on odd numbered days –
for the ability to attract
pickle customers.
On even numbered days –
I will stick to my worship
of climate control.

The Green Burial People
Keep Buying Me Donuts –
Should I Be Worried?

Knock, knock.
We're from the Ace Hardware and Eternal Gardens.
We are here to promote eternal organic resting places
that will better the world's ecological green balance.

Please take this brochure on our raised garden perpetual beds
they will feed a family of four summer after summer
you know.
And with proper maintenance
via our perpetual sprinkler system
you could find yourself providing a surplus
to the local farmers' market.

Mortality equals immortality with
perpetual voice activated headstone ads.
We provide them for your memorialization
as our new option feature.
AARP approves of our Resting Family Cash-flow option
you know.

Please accept these complimentary donuts for listening to us.
Is there coffee? And a guest Wi-Fi password?

Our predictive software
puts you in the 95th percentile for our services
in the next ten years. We have recently acquired
the golf course
behind your house and the raised beds are now up for option.
Wouldn't you love to be an ecological part of your fairway?
You can reserve one or several heirloom beds
with a family discount.

Think of the produce your family could enjoy
for years to come.
We will stay in touch
and please have another cruller with our compliments.
In fact, if you have watch parties for our streaming channel
you will never lack
for these delicious glazed treats evermore.

Remember, a bed today is peace everlasting
but with radishes.
Picture yourself becoming part of the legal weed trade.
How much pleasure you will be providing the family
and friends
as they circle and share your new peace in green oneness.

Also, we provide lawn signs for the front yard proclaiming
your participation in the green ever after.
Reserve now, and we will provide your first year's
germinated seedlings.
Which will include a floral tribute in your initials.

Knock, knock. We're from the Neptune Society.
Has the word reached you
about our seaside kelp bed
and lobster trap eternal resting places?
Imagine drawn butter, thermidor and bisque,
for only a three-year contract.
Yes, we do put the under in undertaker
and you will be top shelf
on the Continental Shelf.
Please accept these complimentary Neptune bibs.

Holiday, with Remembered Scent –
for that Damn Empty Chair

We return from boxing up
our losses
only to discover the lost loved one
seated at our table
gabbing with our friends
smiling
open armed, as we approach –
that now familiar embrace
hidden sighs
joined in stories
and toasts, mindful
of the ghostly arm
around our shoulders.

It Happened in Vegas

You cannot hold me responsible
it happened in Vegas.
Yes, there are Vegas's outside of Nevada
maybe not Las Vegas's
the Las isn't so important now is it?
Legally speaking and I'm talking about a technicality
any Vegas, within its confines, boundaries
and territorial limits will and shall be considered
"...a place where what happens, stays there
in perpetuity and for all intents and purposes of the law
shall be considered a null event..." to be disregarded
by any and all juries, grand or local.
So you see, my geographic defense holds
since the neighboring pub is squarely within
the Vegas naming convention.
Jimmy Vega's Grill and After Hours Pub
has a legal standing
as stipulated by all maps and manner of cartography.
You must unlock this door and let my drunk ass in.

Spending the Day with a Fine Thought

It came to mind
out of left field
with a say-cheese smile
nothing was to be done about it
but appreciate it for what it was
a fine thought
a not-small thought
hidden in or
hidden behind
a most ordinary thought

something like a found thing you might
toss or bat about
bounce and catch off a wall several times

not fleeting at all
nor disappearing with harsh distraction
not demanding attention undivided
but its slightest touch or nudge
returned whole
the stray inner smile.

This fine thought did not leave
but floated to and fro
always in reach, sometimes deep
in a pocket
content with either movement or tarry

a guiltless positive
an uplift like warm rain
in full sunlight or
naked stillness of absent breeze.

You know this yourself
from a satisfying thought of your own
hanging about
simple as two plus two.

It was nice spending that time with
such a fine thought
that brought such a fine inner smile
for the best part of all that day.

When You Consider Yourself Learned

What are you going to know and how conventional
will your wisdom be
by the time you own it
when the learning stage peaks
will you know
how to beat the stock market
how to hold your liquor.

Will you know the difference
between the sacred and the profane
knowing convention hides each in the other's garb
between a friend and an enemy holding you closer
than your real friends
between the republic and the republicans
between democracy and the democrats
between your ass and all the holes in Albert Hall.

Is it a matter of what you want
when you no longer want anything.

What role do you think unimaginable trauma will play
in the rest of your life
careful again
there are silver linings to starting over
what role will horrendous loss play
what role will your worst judgment play.

How much regret can you stand
when you meet it coming the other way and recognize it
how much of that regret can you wall off
how much of that regret will lower your expectations
how much of that regret remains
from when you underestimated the competition.

When does your reach balance out
when does the power of incrementalism hit you
when does falling down not hurt anymore
when does the center hold
when does the center fold.

I see
you do not have a clue
welcome to the least exclusive club in the universe
you're seated with the greatest minds of your generation
wish we could do better for you
but it's a crowded house these nights
the band is sweet oblivion
they take requests
feel free
but please we beg you
do not to go to the restrooms unescorted.

Left in the Lurch

The bus has a mad driver
the wheels screech
the driver is breaking every rule of the road
he swerves right and left
we passengers hang on and
wonder what has got into him today
if we could read minds
we would know his girlfriend was
kissing a stranger in the rear seat.
The driver is successful at keeping them apart.
He reminds me of every god
I've ever prayed to.

Music Box Ballerina

With every push
of the switch
opening of the box

I believe
you love
what you do.

Otherwise
you must be
a Tiny Psycho Dancer.

And that makes me
very afraid.

My Vincent Price Dream

I woke and my wife was gone
in her place a cooing dove sat on her pillow.
A dove, I thought.
When you transitioned
I had expected
a talkative raven, no?

The dove cooed
and looked at me with
questioning eyes –
what had I done to her?
Talking in my sleep
had I let a spell fall on her?
A faulty 'I love you, my dove'
in the heat of passion.

Ah sweet Lenore
I beg your forgiveness
while I search out a spell of mercy.
I searched my books
of incantations and magical dances
that I might bring her back to me
which was when Lennie walked in to ask
what's that bird doing here?
I told you to close the windows
not keep them open.
She grabbed that innocent bird
and placed it on the sill.
I thought wait, let me go too –
please ...

Out with the Old – Never Really Happens

That holiday call home
is a little different this year.

I cannot say
put the old man on
tell him
some made up small talk stuff
about the bulls
the cubs
the bears
the weather
his garden
or his great grandkids
who screamed around his chair
doing great grandkid things
like the airplanes in King Kong.
Out with the old
never
really happens.

The new dive
gleefully on top
then go
their distracted way.

Procrastination Marks

I have no idea what they are
but when I come to one my feet are stuck in tar
pretty clever way to handle unfinished writing
I go outside and take up kiting
I get like a honey-fingered baby with a feather
I put a word down and there I'm tethered.

A writer with no met deadlines
creates few articles and headlines.

Here I am stuck for one word or another
and there's a breeze blowing through
from one ear to the other.
My mind starts to roam
when a procrastination mark
pops me right out of a story.

I'd give you an example
but it's hard to put into words
when I'm stuck looking out a window
at some fascinating bird.

Calendar pages pile up
while I try for just the right word.
It's a writer's lot to figure such things
tied with a bow only neater.
Advice to those who use a procrastination mark
to keep their place.

They're an excellent way
to watch a beard take over your face
If there ever was a better "waste of time"
to stop a clock, or marching band mid-step
quicksand for act and scene.

These marks
like upside down and sideways
Greek letters cast a spell.
Their purpose
to make an editor's life
a living hell.

Pickup Line

Sure, I'm in a band.

Well
we had a practice
last spring.

Cover songs
but we plugged in
and everything.

Snail Shakespeare

What's in the water these days
animals are getting so smart
squirrels are doing mazes and
jumping off spinning discs
to counter-weighted
planks to ropes with pulleys.

Birds are making stick tools to get bugs
cats are throwing food off counters to dogs
that can't get up that high.
They're figuring out door handles.
My own bird rings his bell
when he wants the light off.
Koko got famous for sign language.
Whales thank divers for cutting nets
they're entangled in.

Next I presume
snail slime sonnets or scientific formulas?
Barbershop quartets with dogs howling?
Postcards from runaway pets?
Goldfish semaphore?
And when the plants catch up –
will I have to turn them away from TV's Jeopardy
to get my wrong answer heard for a change?
Damn snickering pansies …

They'd Have You Believe

The world is half good
and half evil
but walking where they say evil lives
there's more smoke than fire.

Eat the food
see the sights
delve
delving is what it's all about.

From the west side of Chicago
to whatever the wrong side of the tracks is in your city
go for the poetry echoing from the buildings
from the walls of the expressways
from the storefronts that revolve between upscale and down.

Vigilante angel subway riding cadre
like the herd with an eye to the predators loping alongside
to the center from where the directives radiate.

Business as usual
until it isn't
and it's your haunch in the predator's mouth
and your eyes are large in disbelief.

Immunity in numbers is no immunity at all
learn the danger signs
heed the signals not the noise.

If you live for the journey
there's nowhere to land.
If you live for the destination
there's only the last breath that matters.

Find your path
delve
as strange a word as ever existed.

Delve deeper
there's more beyond
most of which
you aren't meant
to know.

Why In Hell – Yerington Nevada
for Gene Bloom, Arthur Winfield Knight, and Pat Hickerson

Gene –

had ugly sloppy junkie bruises
all around the catheter needle in his arm.
His nursing home help looked Haitian.
His mind was consumed with a roll call of visitors
he asked about people who hadn't come to see him off
surprised by some who did.
Thought maybe she'd come too but no luck there.

I took him to the track a last time
before all this came down and
he gave me horses that are still out there.
He laughed through his pain.
He laughed hard like he did at the last open mic we did
around his hospital bed.

Arthur –

in Yerington Nevada –
Why in hell's name did Arthur and Kit move to that
dusty two casino high plains nowhere town
halfway between a somewhere
and an anywhere?

Arthur looked tired of fighting
but wouldn't let any doctor near him
so a woman doctor came –
maybe he thought she was a nurse?
On our last visit, Kit said he wouldn't talk to us
face to face.
Talk to him from the hallway
was the only way.

Door closed
leaning against the wall
we said we were leaving
but we double backed
to catch him out on the living room couch.

When the call comes
you say the expected things
because you're expected
to be saying them.

Pat –

Pat Hickerson fooled me.
She was productive all the way.
No tell in her eyes, no tell in her voice.
Some people knew –
we didn't.
We should have
but we didn't.

Geography of the dying outlaw
is all of this – is the sum of this
contains such places as Yerington Nevada
dusty way-stops on those stretched-out high plains
prone to snow they're not supposed to have.
A cold dry place, meaning excellent for storage –
which in the end explains –
Why in hell – Yerington Nevada?

The Trade

In my 70s
I will trade for someone's 20s from the 90s
knowing these 21st century teen years
I want the money from my country club 50s
and the never sick a day health of my 40s.

I now ride a battery powered bike up hills
the same grades I shot up in my pre-teens
with sheer desperation of being late for the game.
The root beer stand logo on my uniform
orange hand-me-down stirrup socks with
rubber bands for the stretched out elastic
leg muscles digging for uphill speed.

When the 60s were more than music
more than Camelot
more than French lessons
more than even that delivery room vigil
more than Marvel comics
and more than family Sunday dinners.

Trade you straight up all the way to the cellular.
All the way to the same nightly moon and stars.
All the way to what is waiting in tomorrow's darkness.

Yes, I want some ballplayer's prime
where his eye can see the seams
and his arms can put the bat hard on that fastball.
I would trade these golden years knowing
my wife, child and grandchild have everything in hand.
For the days and years ahead, when like my Mother –
I'm granted 80s and 90s due to leaping medical advances
I'll become that kid again.
Happy to be doing what I did again
Playing ball, in orange hand-me-down stirrup socks.

All Donations Accepted

At the safari themed enclosure
I bought oranges to feed the elephants
asked a khaki dressed staff member
what I could buy to feed the tiger.

The attendant said come here a sec.
He took hold of my short-sleeved arm
where he made a sharpie mark at my elbow.
Just put your arm through his bars up to there.

I am going to pretend that did not happen.
The tiger hung his head, disappointed
at my lack of charity.

After Hours Bond Girl

She –
the blonde
of many
hard years.

A toll
on the beauty
that once was.

Owned the
end bar stool
at the country club.

If you got
too close

spent any time
near her or got curious

you heard she was
more than acquainted
with bond –
not just bonded booze
but James Bond
the original one.

Fantasy
or fact she wrote poetry
about it.

To the rest of us
it was something
that would never
let her go.

We didn't
get too close –
but the story
never got old
nor the poetry
from the girl
of gold.

Nothing but a Number

When you feel the grip of the reaper
on the elbow and the urge to kick loose
one uppermost in mind
remember that the call is not
a gentle guiding
or a cautionary sign.
Time is up.
The finish line is the windshield and you
you are the bug.
It is best to go along to
the next party, the next gathering.
The clouds are parting for your climb
and the earth is open to swallow your soul.
Either way, it wouldn't hurt to ask for
another cup of coffee, or another sip of tea before
the journey. The reaper himself might join you.
Only do not challenge him to a wager
to save your mortal life. The reaper has seen
them all. You would have to cheat
and the reaper will reverse any good fortune you
had waiting if caught.
He has seen them all.
However, we know of one winning avenue –
a Beach Boys listening contest.
You and Death might get to walk around
for quite a while humming Kokomo.
Your life insurance company
thanks you in advance.

An Anthropological Apology

Up in age looking around, we inhabit
a desert university dig far below
feeling connected to the old ones
of history and the old ones unrecorded.
Strange connections with names
on many tombs in many foreign places
like past lives we've lived – and might
even live again.
Lives without histories, too.
Only names and dates with imagination
to fill in the lives between the dates.
These graveyards tell time for them and announce
that some of them lived to questionable maturity.
But my connection is now deeper, more certain
of relationships along centuries. Here we are, two old gods
talking of having been to Disneyland; there is a
bond of having lived many times, both parallel and
intersecting.
Old souls, old energy, old acquaintances
with the ticket to the system called being born.
Spirits in touch with the rude candy land of existence.
We had walked the plank, installed ourselves in the bellies
of mothers, and found nothing to joke about.
One hell of a ride, existence. We consider doing it again
a few thousand years up the line. But this time
I want to be the zookeeper. The other can be the Messiah.
When you are the Chosen One they never leave you alone.
Or worse.

Balloons

The life one leads
has a happy ending
and is not cheated
if one goes out
like an untied balloon.
Loosed
and escaping.
Too fast for the eye.

Bar Talk in B

Kind of dead tonight.
Big show somewhere else
want to split.
Sure
but
you're headlining.
Oh, yeah.

How to Keep a Friend

On the assumption no news
is good news
I let a long, deep friendship
lapse.
My friend thought
I was not
interested
I hadn't stayed in touch.

What was your name again?
Your birthday?
Now I take notes.
When is a good time to call?
Does co-signing a loan
sound complicated to you?

Boney Maroney, Sloopy,
and the Plan from Outer Space

Five thousand fingers of death
crowded the gymnasium while
our stockinged feet felt the poetry in motion.
Johnny B. Goode turned into Van Helsing.
We were afraid the vampires we were promised
were no-shows until the motorcycles roared
through the doors in a parade of blood.

We tightened up with filet gumbo from
the Wolfman and ignored the bayou creature.
It danced the night away picking off wallflowers.
The bobbysoxer wouldn't let go of the mummy's leg
as he bumped her down the steps and into the night.
The thing about the twist was "how low could you go."
Tinglers, ghosts, and man-faced dogs shouted
"Give me an M!" which was a clue to shake it Moni Moni.

Fashion maven in suede shoes
and "Chantilly Lace" – Cronos
himself led the chamber in the encore performance of
"This Diamond Ring" is going to keep on shining
for me and my
queen of the damned rodeo and rocking jailhouse chairs.
Homecoming turned into home-going as the dancers
twisted a final dance.
Saw what you did last summer to the fading strains of
bedpost chewing gum, beach blankets
and purple people eating
tarantula monsters from the "Ninth Planet." Good times, said
the bloody "Red Baron" about his missing monster, Sloopy.

The Callback

I don't telephone Los Angeles friends.
Their blood pressure is already too high.
They equate the ring of the phone
with news from God
that they're special after all.
They'd get bothered
if the grim reaper was at the doorbell.
One told Death, No, no, can't
I am due at a callback.
Death, it is reported, said
Wow. Two in one day!

Bar Talk in D

Hey, who's the band?
Let's see
the outlaws
drummer from halfway house
lead guitar from the street
(with warrants)
singer from rehab
bass from county.
Yep
that's them all right
not a half bad bill
all friends
with musical issues
and ankle jewelry.

Mid-Life Punk

Babies
jobs and spouses
bosses and co-workers
potlucks and casual days
dress up presentations.
Early morning flights
with late night returns.

Meals and family time
TV, popcorn bowl, togetherness.
Read a real book two months ago.
Now, all I read are the business articles
in the weekly.

The promotion looks like it will happen
and that noose will fit like a glove.
Rainbow spiked hair and piercings
so very far away now.

But I will hire
a very surprised one
tomorrow.
Fill the spot I left.
A dream
long in waiting.

Bookie Blues

I'll beat the dead eight horse
I bet on today
if you wake the corpse
that rode him that way.

Caused me no little burn
when she stopped for a portrait at the turn
and the jockey saw them all making so much dust
as I went bust.

It was not just the pose
that caused the loss by a lot more than a nose.

I knew gone was my handsome wager
when midrace he answered his pager.

So for me the sport of kings
is gone the way of many things
but now the pressure is on me
the check I bet with was, um, rubbery.

Bus Ride Next To an Unfettered Mind

She is a little one with
a consistent bent for exaggeration
that yields tiny people
and two-story tall poodles
fuzzy birds and feathery turtles
underground circuses with acrobatic poets.
Her school is on a different planet
that is so tiny she is the only student
but it does have a forest of mean ducks on the way
but it's okay because her horse has long legs.
She is pretty sure that when she grows up
she will know the words to every song
so she can sing along with the tall dancing mice
on her afternoon television program
her program, starring her, of course.
She has to do a homework poem about her bus ride.
I tear off my notebook page
hand her back her words.
She thinks I'm funny because
she can do so much better.

The Wish

She rubbed the lamp
wished her only wish

with the gentleness
her mother used
so long ago

the genie
brushed her hair.

Bike Rider Pedaling into Tomorrow

Two of my uncles
unboxed the television at grandmother's house.
I heard all my aunts and uncles
had gone in on the first family color TV.
I took my girlfriend there to watch that new color TV.
We rode our bikes down the tree lined streets to Gram's
to that spectacular round picture
in a large square box on short legs.
Some shows tinged green – some tinged red –
orange alien people
but at least the vertical hold worked so
it was a new world
a brand new world where
heartache and grief were a thing of the past.
When you have gone from "Gunsmoke" on the radio
to "George Reeves' Superman" on black and white TV
and now there was color
and cowboys across the range
life was too amazing not to think other impossible things.
Might be a few "Flash Gordon" tomorrows away.
It was Camelot and the space race was on.
When the riderless horse tethered to the caisson
and Kennedy's son's salute dashed it all to hell for decades
we cried like children.
Just a few "Flash Gordon" tomorrows
away from a happy bike ride on a tree lined-street.

Evan "Mikey" Myquest is a poet, writer, and Cubs fan married for 45 years to his Swiss-German wife, Eva. They live near Sacramento, CA and are known for being café art and music patrons. Myquest was born in North Central Illinois, grew up on the pulp science fiction and mystery magazines of the day, and in 1974 attended the Clarion Science Fiction and Fantasy Workshop at Michigan State University. His instructors included Harlan Ellison, Thomas M. Disch, and Damon and Kate Knight. His poetry has appeared alongside Leonard Cohen, Lawrence Ferlinghetti, Jack Hirschman, Patti Smith, Jim Carroll, and Ann Menebroker. In 2017, a tribute documentary video by Susana Halfon featuring his poetry was premiered at the Crocker Art Museum in Sacramento.

Made in the USA
Columbia, SC
02 October 2020